C0-BJJ-891

Tales of My Grandmothers

A Story by
Jeanne W. Carey

PublishAmerica
Baltimore

© 2007 by Jeanne W. Carey.
All rights reserved. No part of this book may be reproduced, stored in a retrieval system or transmitted in any form or by any means without the prior written permission of the publishers, except by a reviewer who may quote brief passages in a review to be printed in a newspaper, magazine or journal.

First printing

At the specific preference of the author, PublishAmerica allowed this work to remain exactly as the author intended, verbatim, without editorial input.

ISBN: 1-4241-9754-6
PUBLISHED BY PUBLISHAMERICA, LLLP
www.publishamerica.com
Baltimore

Printed in the United States of America

Dedication

This is affectionately dedicated to all those who have special Grandmothers who made the memories of their childhood warm and merry. I had two bright spots in my life that gave my growing years treasures to remember.

Acknowledgment

These tales would stay just memories dimmed in time if it were not for my daughter, Cathy. Her encouragement and help brought them into print. "A tale not told dies" Irish saying.

Contents

Chapter 1—Introduction

Grandmothers are great additions to family life. They are the connection that binds the family together. When we were little, they were people we visited on Sunday. We always expected candy or cookies, even when mom said we couldn't have any and gave in when she agreed on just one piece. They would hug us and laugh at our stories. When they didn't cook we would go out to eat at a restaurant and that was fun except we had to mind our manners and sit up straight. Sometimes when we would stay overnight, wonderful stories would be told about what they did when they were little and about their mother and father. Looking back now as the past was and how we felt about life, we were only concerned that they loved us and we knew it.

My Grandmothers were fascinating. One came from Russia Poland and whose history was one that was fraught with tales of terror and fright that only wars can bring on. Wolves, raids and escapes completed her life. The other grandmother was one of daring do that defied the laws of averages and her firm conviction that nothing was impossible when she was in the right. Her beliefs stemmed from her Irish Catholic background and her determination to succeed.

My Irish Grandmother, Mary Elizabeth Kelly and the other was my Polish Grandmother, Marianna Ezbieta Kozloska. I called the first one "Kelly" or "Kell" because everyone else referred to her that way. Marianna was always "Grammy" to me. Kelly said she was too young to be a "granny" while Grammy was quite old when I was born. No matter, between the two of them, I found the sparkle of full living in the lives of these precious people.

Kelly was a red-haired, blue-eyed, rounded, five foot two inch container of excitement. She was never still and generated tremendous energy. She moved quickly, talked, laughed and enjoyed her days as a veritable whirlwind of activity. The gift of tongues given her and her ability to project her feelings and attitudes were monumental. Kelly's wild sense of humor was better suited to the stage than the mundane setting of our city.

In complete contrast, Grammy was a quiet lady. She dressed her short ample body in dresses that came to just three inches above the floor and always wore an apron girdling her roundness. White hair pulled up into a bun topped her classic peasant face. The most arresting features she had were a pair of very blue eyes and a cute little smile. These brought all the soft wrinkles into such a pleasant arrangement that all the years seem to fade in the vitality of her expression. The strength and dignity of her years played a sweet accompaniment to the spontaneous and childlike delight in the love she had for people. She was warm and gentle, and was different from many of the other grandmothers I knew. She laughed and smiled a lot.

I was very much loved by both of these women and each in their own way contributed to my growing-up. I was blessed. This is a collection of the stories they told. The events that I witnessed and the funny things I saw that they did or said. Of course, they have become gold-touched by the years, but all did happen and the tales have been told and retold.

Kelly's attitude was best said in Latin, "Illegitimi non Carborundum," or "Don't let the bastards get you down." She had an indomitable will to succeed no matter what. God was her champion. She laughed a lot in defiance of the world she lived in. I think in those early days tending bar as a teenager in her father's saloon formed her gifts for quick wit and spontaneous repartee. She absorbed much about life between the "growlers" of beer and the men she served.

Kelly with her sister and her mother took over the bar after her father died. He died of consumption at the age of 35. The bar was located down in the poor section of town call "Gander Bay."

Kelly was so social and she never lost her ability to engage in a sprightly duel of words just for the pure joy it gave her. She could always find a solution to a problem and never hesitated to take a chance. This accounted for her successes.

Grammy was different. If she ever had a motto or thought of one, it would be, "Hope is always there." She believed that everything would turn out all right. I have a picture in my heart of her sitting near the window telling her beads with reverence. The only time I saw tears in her eyes, was when she prayed that fateful day in September in 1939. I just came home from school and she was sitting with the newspaper on her lap, rosary in her hand and tears in her eyes. The headlines in great letters spoke the disaster "Poland invaded by Germany." I hugged her. She asked me to read it to her. I did and changed some of the words so she would understand. This was just one of the sorrows of her very eventful life. The hardships she lived through were extraordinary but her hopeful trust carried her through the events of tumultuous times. I think this is why she lived so long.

These two complimented each other. One was passionate the other passive. They could switch back at times, but the motivating ability was their wonderful adjustments to the times of their lives. They were survivors.

I have told these tales randomly without regard to chronological order except for the introductions and epilogue.

Chapter 2—
Grammy's Early Life—A Beginning

From the records, she was born in June 3, 1856, in the village of Saniki, Poland. Her proper name was "Mary Elizabeth Zembrowski." The date is a little different from my mother's knowledge, but Grammy lied about her age, so who knows? I think she didn't want the authorities to refuse to give her a passport due to her age. She never had an uneventful life. I was told how she hid in the cornfields from the Cossacks (Russian elite military), during attacks on her village. Being small and quick, she would huddle down into such a tiny bundle that she evaded detection even though she was but four feet from the soldiers. Close by, an unfortunate villager was tortured and cried out for help. She dared not go to his aid lest she was discovered. The waiting for him to stop his screaming or die must have been terrible. At one point, she cautiously lifted her head up to see whether the Cossacks had left and a woman jumped up from her hiding place and ran out with a babe in her arms. Upon seeing her, a horseman ran her down and cut her head off with his saber. The head rolled to the ground, the torso took a few steps, and then fell on the infant. Grammy said she buried the little body along side its mother later that day.

In her teens she married a coachman, Tomas Kosloski, much against her family's wishes. I think the objections were that the man of her choice was not known in the village. She could read and write and was a teacher to the noble families. Grammy also came from a well-known, established family. However, Tomas Kosloski new nothing about himself, his mother or his father. He was brought up in an orphanage. From what my mother has said, Tomas was a very strong, dark complexion young man, about six feet tall and had piercing dark blue eyes. The marriage was a happy one and she had three children rather early. Later on she had a son Frank and at fifty-two, she bore my mother, Jana. My mother said that her dad was so proud of her. Carrying her around on his shoulders, Tomas never stopped bragging about his Janina (little Jeanne).

At many times in their tumultuous life, progroms would spread across Russia. These were systematic killing of Jews. A decree would issue forth and then the soldiers came. Tomas and Grammy contrived ways to hide their friends until the persecutions ceased. They had special trees at the southern end of the island they owned. Each tree had a cache of food and blankets stored carefully at its base. The fortunate who managed to swim to the island undetected were assured food and warmth. Jews, if found on your land, were killed. Jail was a penalty for helping them. There was a system of warning signals. Grandma and her husband were fortunate. They escaped detection and saved many. Grammy said that after a progrom, some Jews kissed the hem of my grandfather's garments in the street.

One time proved too much. The Russians killed so many Jews, the dangers of pestilence arose. The decree from the Czar was that any man who owned over two horses was conscripted for duty to bury the Jews. Tomas had to go. He was away for some time and came back with sickening stories. His appetite was gone, sick at heart, mind and body, he died within two years. Before his death, he worried about the political upheaval in the country and the possibility of revolution. He urged his son to leave for America to escape conscription. With the help of his Jewish friends, he managed to have Frank leave without any resistance. With just a few months left to him, Tomas settled all his affairs. He relied on his friends to help his wife and Janina who was about ten, to escape. The borders were closed. Only the bribery and extra greasing of palms helped them through Germany, France and on the Liverpool. Then they came to America. Grammy was actually sixty-six years old and ready to start a new life.

Chapter 3—A Wolf Story

Grandmother came-up from the farm and would stay with us for a few of the hard winter months. The days always took on a special glow. She baked a lot of bread, made me my favorite dishes and babied me. It was during these times, the quiet moments after school that she would talk the most. I always asked her for stories of the old country, when I found out that she were not born here. I was fascinated. In my narrow life, I assumed that everybody was an American and all spoke English. Here my Grammy spoke broken English, and had lived in Poland-Russia. I was always quizzing her about her growing up and what it was like. I begged her for stories.

Grammy told me two wolf stories that had me wild-eyed with excitement and fear. They were surely different from anything I could have imagined happening. Albany, New York, was so civilized. The only thing left for exploring were the vacant lots down the street, the birch-grove and the swamp. There was also an old Indian who lived in back of the convent and made souvenirs, but he wasn't very frightening. We had to stretch our imagination to ever think of Indian raids or the "Last of the Mohicans" after being with him for an afternoon. The thought of living where wolves roamed, delighted and scared me all at the same time.

The first story she told me came after my asking her what life was like when she was growing up. Did she do the same things I did? Grammy smiled and said "Not always, some things were very different. For instance, there were wolves and many dangers at times." Then she told me a wolf story.

Grammy as a teenager was one of the few in her village to read and write. (How this came about, I do not know) Anyway being literate, she was in demand as a tutor for the children of the nobility. Now the estates were some distance from her village and the walk was long. She had received a new, very fashionable parasol to protect her from the sun. She was proud of her birthday gift, using it daily on her visits to the great homes.

At one point in her travels, she had to pass through a rather dense forest that, except from small patches of sunlight that darted down to the forest floor, was quite dark and gloomy. This wood was part of the noble's lands and just before the estate. She hurried through the shaded pathway and saw a dead horse lying on its side. She gingerly stepped past it, with its cloud of flies swarming around the swollen belly. It probably belonged to one of the family members. They were a careless lot and most undoubtedly ran the horse to death and just left it.

The day was uneventful. Grammy taught the children and was heading home once more. The sun was getting low in the sky and she feared the woods. No one in their right mind would travel a forest path at night because wolves roamed freely. She didn't need her parasol open now so she folded it and started through the trees.

Grammy remembered the dead horse with disgust. Just as she came in view of it, it moved. Rather the stomach moved. She stood still and watched the belly rise and fall and contort. A dark object appeared at the lower part of the stomach. She realized it was a wolf and he had been eating the entrails of the horse, having torn a large hole in the horse's midsection. The animal was three-quarters of the way inside eating eagerly. Grammy froze. She was terrified! Without any further thought, she decided to detour around the horse and the wolf. As she made her way through the underbrush by the side of the road, she stepped on a dead branch that snapped with a loud crack. The wolf backed out of the carcass and she found herself looking at a yellow-eyed enormous creature with blood dripping jaws. She did the only thing she could think of, that was to take her parasol and snap it open. The wolf let out a screech, leaping in the air and falling over the horse. He was dead. Grammy was in a state of shock. She just folded her parasol and ran the rest of the way to the village.

Her Dad told her later that the men checked the wolf and decided the beast had gorged himself. The sudden opening of the parasol caused him to leap in

15

the air in fright and the violent strain was too much for his bloated body. The wolf had punctured something inside.

The story always made me breathless. I lived every part of it. I never asked her anymore about it, no badgering for extra details. It was all there and terrifying.

Chapter 4—

Introduction to Kelly—Another Beginning

Mary Elizabeth Kelly was born sometime in the 1870's. Her father was born and raised in Ireland. He said his family's home was next to the cottage of the farmhouse singer, John McCormick in Athlone. Mike Kelly came to America and ended up in Albany. He had a bar in Gander Bay and served all his fellow compatriots until consumption took him. His widow ran the bar after that and her two young daughters helped her. Kelly and her sister Josephine served the customers under mother's watchful eyes. They were both completely family oriented and were close to each other until death separated Kelly from her sister. I believe both met their husbands while serving beer. I know Kelly did. She met Charles there and he was sorely smitten. Asking for her hand in marriage, her mother turned him down. She had felt Kelly was not ready, had not matured and was too young. "Shorty" Charles nickname, pressed his suit for three years, finally her mother assented to the union. There was a small marriage in the church and the two went to New York on their honeymoon. There was one glitch; mother had never told her about the facts of life. Kelly raised such a rumpus in the hotel room; the hotel detective was called in as well as the police. Kelly was battling Shorty and was winning. It was all resolved when Shorty's sister Aunt Mae, came in from Long Island to calm her down and help her understand. Poor Kelly's education into adult life was traumatic.

To the best of my knowledge, Josephine, her sister, met her husband at the bar as well. He was a fireman and in those days of horse drawn engines, he manned the hook and ladder with the big draft horses. He was a large man with a lot of strength. People said he was magnificent the way he handled those massive horses in the race to the fire.

The families were close, Kelly had three boys and Josephine had one girl. Shorty had this tremendous love of the theatre and eventually became a stage manager. He started as a stage carpenter and worked his way up. Being very well educated, Shorty introduced Kelly to his culture and traditions, which soon became part of her own. The finished product was a dynamic personality, well spoken, well informed, with the Irish charm that was so beguiling. Kelly was a character and a delightful grandmother.

Chapter 5—The Age Factor

Kelly was always bedeviled by the age factor. She had her three boys very young. All three boys were in the public eye; Harry, my father, and Roger were lawyers and Charlie was on the west coast writing scripts. (Kelly always appeared to be younger than she actually was.) With this in mind, she played her age numbers like a riverboat gambler played with crooked dice. Whatever age was necessary, she used it. I think it was the very busy life she led, and it seemed her zest for living sprung from some magical fountain of energy.

Kelly was in complete denial of her age when I showed up as her first grandchild. Maybe in her mind she was a child bride and my Dad was a teenager who just graduated from law school as a child genius with me in his arms. Actually, Dad was twenty-one when he received his law degree and Mom was eighteen when I was born. This was the first age factor that comes to mind. Kelly was too young to be a grandmother. The news shell-shocked her. As a lovely red-haired beauty,"Grandmother meant old to her...very old." She equated the term with the age and looks of my other grandmother, who looked like a traditional "grandmere." She wore her gray-white hair in a soft bun, had soft wrinkles and wore a long dress that denied any shape to her but fullness in the chest area. Kelly was horrified at the prospect of "grand motherhood"

She didn't hate children but the thought of my birth was out of some natural order she had in mind. Perhaps she pictured a wealthy woman in her late fifties welcoming the advent of a grandson with joy. Well, I bounced in and upset the schemes of her dreams, priorities and plans. And to top it off,

I was a girl. Her thought was that the first grandchild had to be a boy. It all worked out eventually. I was the only girl in my generation for twenty-plus years, so I was special.

However she insured against the chances of her age becoming known by forbidding my brother and I from calling her grandma. She made sure that Harry (my brother) called her "Kelly." This was her maiden name. Even my mother called her "Kelly," which was more formal as a ladies name. For reasons known only to the happy vacant minds of children, the name "Kelly" fit her and stuck all through the years. I doubt whether we could ever equate Mary Elizabeth Kelly Williams with our "Kelly" in our younger years. It was great to yell "Kelly, look at us," when we were sleigh riding down the hill. And we felt protective when calling her name to tell her to watch out for the bump, then to see her bounce off the toboggan into the soft snow. The "Age Factor" was O.K. with us…and having "Kelly" around us was a different grandmother experience.

The next incident was getting a job with the State of New York. How she got it was a "Kelly" happening. I remember her telling me she had only three years of formal schooling. She was quick to learn. I would watch her practice on the typewriter before taking the qualifying test. She passed the test and what she told them regarding other credentials, I haven't the faintest idea. I know she did a very good job for fifteen years and then retired. Not to my credit, I used to go down to her office after school and "Kelly" introduced me as her niece and I know she was very worried that I would tell everybody that she was my grandmother. I recall I was a senior in high school at the time. Looking back, I know she did a shave job on her years, so she would be able to work long enough to collect retirement. She probably felt that if she told her real age, she wouldn't have gotten the job. This was true at that time and I'm a little ashamed I teased her so.

Another time was when she passed her Realtors exam and selling real estate. It was a brave new world for many young women, being a Realtor, and here was "Kelly" with her changeable years selling property and making a living at it. In fact she'd keep my father advised on good buys. Recognizing her uncanny ability to spot good deals, he profited when he bought several parcels on her recommendation. She finally bought a house with her youngest son Roger and she lived there with him and his family for the rest of her life.

This age factor carried right through even with my father's untimely death from a heart attack at Walter Reed Hospital in Washington DC. The obituary with his picture stated that he was in his in his thirties. "Kelly's" fine hand had helped with the vital statistics. Dad was forty-three. This shaving of a few years took a few years off her age as well.

Whatever company she was with at any given time, she was always able to fit in. The people around her thought she was their age or close to it. In her latter years, she'd walk to the neighborhood bar with a friend of hers and they'd swap stories with their friends. She was never at a loss for words except where it came to her age.

I'M TOO YOUNG TO BE A GRANNY

I'm too young to be a Granny
I was told Grannies are old, and
there's no twinkles to their wrinkles.
Their faces are long and without a song.
They're so slow, absolutely no get up and go,
I'm not critical, but most are arthritical,
And I'm too young to be a Granny
I'm young, a few years after my thirties.
Lively and pretty and I'm a wee bit flirty.
Dancing and laughing, I have this to say,
I'm too young to be a granny.

Chapter 6—Grammy as an Immigrant

Grammy was burdened with the loss of her beloved Tomas, her home and a very uncertain future. My mother was young and needed care and Grammy was sixty-six. They left Poland and came through Ellis Island. I asked my mother what it was like; she said "scary." They were packed in with all the other refugees who were escaping from the clouds of war, seeking a better life. Every night, all would gather and dance and sing. Grammy was seasick all the time and when the ship finally landed she was very relieved.

Once through Ellis Island, both ended up in a tenement house, in a section called "Hell's Kitchen" in New York City. It was a slum area on the lower west side of Manhattan, having an unsavory reputation for criminal activity. Now, it was a haven for the hordes of newcomers. There were Greeks, Bulgarians, Polish, Spaniards, Irish, French, Italians and Czechs to name some. My mother said she went to school immediately to learn English. The teacher had the patience of Job. With forty-five in her class, her instructions consisted of holding up an apple and telling them to repeat after her—— aaaaaaa pulllllll. It worked. My mother said after two years she mastered the language. As for Grammy, she did not go to school and learned haphazardly.

They lived in a four-story tenement house, and Grammy stated that the top floor was occupied by Greeks and Bulgarians. The third floor housed several German families, the Irish were on the second and Grammy and mom had the first floor with some Italian folks. One of the most terrifying happening for them both was when they were separated. Mom came home from school to find the flat was empty. No Mom. She waited until dark expecting her any minute.

Night fell and she huddled in a corner with the door bolted. The next morning, she went to school, as she was afraid of the truant officer. She cried each night as she huddled hungry until, the Italian lady across the hall brought her something to eat. The language was a terrible barrier. At the same time, Grammy had taken ill and somebody notified the authorities. She ended up in the hospital in the charity ward ailing and not able to communicate. Finally somebody who could speak Polish helped and found out there was a thirteen year old girl sitting by herself in a flat all alone and with no food. It was a wonderful reunion for both. Mom was able to visit every day and she ate her meals with the Italian family until Grammy came home.

I never did find out what the trouble was and Mom did not know either, but it was a devastating event. Mom said she never wanted to experience such a terror and aloneness again.

Grammy said that nobody had any possessions in that building except for the clothes on their backs, some small treasures and a few pots and pans. Everybody but the Irish were on the second floor. She said they utilized only one pot. Daily it was used for oatmeal, for lunch it served as a soup pot, afternoon it was used for a few growlers of beer, and for the supper meal. After supper it was used as a thunder-mug. The pattern was repeated daily.

Mom said she played with all the other kids. They used to dare each other to jump from the roof of one tenement to the. She stopped after a little boy missed and fell. The ambulance took his broken body away and all the families went to the funeral. The kids played in the streets after that.

Grammy had a time with mom's hair. She had lice constantly, even though her hair was washed daily. She used kerosene to rid her of the little problems. At one point the teacher said that if everybody was free of lice the girls could wear hair ribbons. In the two years, they were no ribbons worn and her daughter's head was always sore from the kerosene.

They met with some Polish people and it was a godsend. As was the custom they acted as match maker and found a widower for Grammy. She moved up to the Catskill Mountains and after a reasonable time of courting, married Jacob. His first wife suffered a stroke while pitching hay on a sweltering summer day. Jake was resolute in his insistence that she should not work in the fields. I think she was very happy with the idea. She was used to working very hard both in the house and yard as well as the fields. It was nice not to work in the fields. He watched over her, cared very deeply for her and never failed to express his feelings. Life was pleasant. She also became an American citizen by virtue of her marriage to Jacob. She was so proud of her citizenship. They worked the farm together. Her son Frank came to live with them so her family was altogether after the years of separation. One miserable winter after a ten year marriage, Jake died with pneumonia.

Chapter 7—Afternoon Tea—The Ritual

Beer was Kelly's forte. She had a notably ritual. After work, she always had a bottle or two. When I was staying with her, my job was to go across the street and get her the beer. She had a regular routine. First she would give me one or two "empties" which she put into a brown paper sack. I was never supposed to let anybody know what she bought as I purchased her beer and gave the bottles for deposit. I got a nickel off for each one. Her pattern continued unerringly as she sat at the table across from me and sipped her beer slowly. The she would talk and talk and talk. It was all about my relatives with their good times and funny things. I was completely fascinated.

It was during one of these times that I learned about the "family" and her relationships with them. One particular incident she told me stands out in my mind. Perhaps it was because it had to do with her beer drinking.

My Grandfather's family were of old colonial stock that had been here since the 1600's. They were accustomed to money and they conserved it. Until the Panic of 1890 when they lost considerable amount of their largess. Anyway, the husband had died and now her mother-in law was alone. It became her custom to travel from North Providence and later Boston in a carriage and four. Over the Old Post road to Albany, New York, was a difficult journey. Kelly told me that she was terrified of her mother-in-law because she represented a life that was so different from her own. Mrs. "W" was a very proper dowager with breeding and the aura of wealth and landed gentry behind her. She would stay for weeks, and sometimes even six weeks. The trip was long and hard in a carriage and required a stopover, so she was not disposed in returning immediately.

Mrs. "W's" letter would come, and Kelly went into a frenzy of excitement. She cleaned and scrubbed every inch of the house, chastised the boys for their manners and sloppiness and made her husband laugh at her antics. He refused to let his mother get him agitated and was amused at his wife's discomfort. He saw no merit in his darling Kelly's upset until he realized there was a problem and it had to do with her beer drinking. At three, Kelly quit whatever she was doing had her beer. Each afternoon, Shorty usually went down to the corner tavern and got a "growler" of beer. Kelly and "Shorty" enjoyed their beer time together. Now Mrs. "W" always had tea at this time, so a plan had to be devised to settle the problem. It worked out well with a scheme of her husband's.

He bought the beer and brought it home. Outside the second story window of the Victorian he would sing an Irish song so she'd know he was there. A rope was lowered by Kelly and he'd secure the container of beer. Of course she would haul it up immediately and pour some in her teacup and return to the table. It meant a few trips back and forth while the ladies chit-chatted about the day and the children. This went on for several years. The friendship between the two women deepened until it was no longer the terrible burden of anxiety that harassed Kelly when her mother-in-law came to visit. On one visit, as Kelly was making the second trip to the little serving room for her drink, Mrs. "W" said, "Kelly, will you give me a little bit of what you are drinking in your teacup on the way back?" A surprised daughter-in-law said "Yes," and brought in the rest of the beer that afternoon tea was fantastic. Kelly was bent over in fits of gaffaws as she told it to me between the giggles and tears of uncontrolled laughter. It seems that "Lydia, Mrs. "W" had known after the first episode what was going on. She said she could not figure out if it was beer or whiskey. Kelly was treated to a story from her mother-in law about her husband and his cronies after a formal dinner, retiring to drink their whiskey and smoke cigars leaving the women to have some tea. The girls decided they should drink too and quietly they started their own sessions. She said the men never knew. She laughed a lot about that tale and Kelly was dumfounded. Shorty came up stairs after hearing all the laughter to join them.

Kelly and Lydia spent many happy hours together after that and enjoyed their teatime. Lydia came to live with them eventually and Kelly took care of her until she died full of years at ninety-four. Until the day she died, Kelly and Lydia always observed their very good tea time.

Beer

Welcome the smile it brings,
happy the heart and mind.
Each sip gives joy to life
and leaves the world behind.

There's laughter in the glass,
and happiness with you.
We've got it all my dear,
let's have another brew.

A cup of kindness,
A cup of brew,
this cup of gladness,
I'll share with you.

Freedom it gives to all,
this splendid drink of ale.
It loosens tongue and heart
to sing and tell a tale.
Many a song unsung,
many a tale untold,
rushes from every glass
to tinge the evening gold.

A cup of kindness,
a cup of brew,
this cup of gladness
I'll share with you.

There's nothing like a bar
where friendship holds you fast.
and all the gang with love,
Talk softly of the past.

Chapter 8—Pea Soup Pistol

All of Grammy's stories were not scary. Some had a twist of humor to them that could give a laugh or a least a smile. One of these was the "Pea Soup Pistol" story. I will call her Mary Elizabeth instead of Grammy, for that was her given name and she was very young then. Anyway she looked out her window one bright morning towards the Polish side. She always differentiated, as the other side was Russian territory. It made no difference that Russia had gobbled up Poland and technically it was all Russia. She held tight to her beliefs, customs and the idea that she lived in Polish territory. She looked casually out the other side and was alarmed to see two boats crossing to her island from the "Russian" side. It meant the police had come to check on them.

The Czar had enacted many new laws over the subjugated area. He was very strict in enforcing them. One law of course was the absolute prohibition of all firearms. Now, Tomas, her husband, had many guns, mostly used for hunting, but he also collected some fine expensive ones for his collection.

Mary Elizabeth hurried out the kitchen door to let Tomas know about the unwelcome visitors to their island. Finding him down near the barn repairing some equipment, she told him. He looked out and to see the boats almost to the landing. Calling to the hired man, they scrambled to hide the unlawful weapons. Mary Elizabeth hid two pistols in the chicken feed and a rifle in the hay very deep down. Putting a few tools scattered around, she hoped it would keep anybody from stabbing into the hay and clinking when the pitchfork struck the metal. The hired man, Jacob, ran to hide his as well. There was no time for using the regular places as they were at the end of the island.

The hated police were now landing and Tomas ran to the house handing the last pistol to Mary Elizabeth telling her to put it someplace in a hurry. Well, she was terrorized as the uniformed men with stern faces came approaching the kitchen door. She plopped the pistol into the pea soup, grabbed the big wooden spoon and stirred. "Good Morning, Pani, may we come in?" She nodded, not trusting herself to talk. The man who was in charge said "The soup smells so good. It is pea soup, is it not?" Mary Elizabeth told him it was. "It's going to be a fine meal today," he said then he directed the men to search the house.

She smelled the warmth of the odors that her soup was creating. It was with pride that she reveled in its goodness. For a brief time she lost herself, scrapping the sides of the great pot carefully pushing the gathering residue from the sides. She watched the swirling mass and the bubbles arise. Yes, it would be a fine meal. She had made bread as well and with the soup, and with some sausage it would be very satisfying. She looked down the hall and realized the men were heading out the back door. She relaxed until she looked down at the pot. The wooden handle of the gun was barely at the surface. It was floating suspended between the very top and the very bottom of the green mass.

The metal part was definitely on the bottom, but the handle was trying to reach the top. It managed to show a dark spot just beneath the first inch of soup. At first glance, one would think it was part of the hambone, but bones do not float. There it was, just enough to arouse the curiosity of anybody. She hit it with a spoon and it answered with a solid sound. She stirred it and it sank momentarily beneath the surface of the swirl. She lifted the spoon and waited. Back to the top came the gun. Shots of panic returned as the thoughts ran rampant through her mind. Where were they now? It was only a few minutes since she saw them leaving the house. She left the soup and went to the window. She watched them as they headed for the barn. Perhaps she should take the gun out now and hide it someplace else. Yes, that's what she should do while they were in the barn. Maybe the flour bin would be a good place. They had already been here and would not look again.

Mary Elizabeth grabbed the spoon and was trying to coax the gun to the side to raise it when a form filled the doorway of the kitchen. She looked up to see the Commandant standing there with a smile on his face. Her heart almost stopped as she stirred. "Ah Pani, the soup smelled so good even out

29

there in the barn. I was drawn to its wonderful aroma. The men are finishing up the inspection and I thought I would come back. Do you think I could have a small bowl of your soup?" With a stunned stutter she managed to say 'Yes' Trying to get a bowl and stir at the same time to hide the gun did not work. The gentleman reached over and took the spoon gently from her to help her serve and immediately the pistol arose. He hit it with a spoon and then managed to retrieve it from the soup.

The rest is history. Before an hour had passed, poor Tomas was on his way to jail on the Russian side, and was not to return for six months. That was the penalty for hiding and having arms. Jacob was there to help her but for that length of time they had to manage without Tomas. The Commandant was still very pleasant and did finish his soup, before he left with her husband.

Chapter 9—Three on a Raft

Kelly was fortunate to have three sons, Harry, Roger and Charlie. The names had a little ring to them, especially when Kelly would call all three when she meant just one of them.

The boys were born about the turn of the century, Charlie was the oldest, my father came next and then there was little Roger. They tried Kelly's patience to the limit daily. My father used to say, mimicking his mother, "Take care of little Rog." Well, they did except for one time, when his guardian angel intervened, here's the story as I heard it.

Kelly was tied up with the managing of the rooming house and it was summertime. The two oldest wanted to play baseball over in the corner lot. Their mother said "No, Rog could get hurt with the ball." Complaining they could not have any fun with him along, Kelly told them they would find something and dismissed them. The two oldest thought of the river and the docks at the wharf. It was hot on the wharf and interesting sailors telling tall tales. It was great fun. They even did a bit of fishing. However, the heat of the day was upon them and the water was beckoning.

Charlie found a raft tied to one of the pilings and it was next to the ladder. What luck! They managed to get little Roger down, by lowering him down to Charlie. Making a pillow for the little guy by using their clothes, they gave him his bottle. He soon was asleep and then they gave themselves up to complete enjoyment of the day. They dove, swam, and splashed each other until they were exhausted. Then they laid on the raft in the sun and rested.

The afternoon sun was benevolent and warmth was pleasant. As the day wore on and shadows blocked the sun rays, it started to get a little cool. At the same time, there was a voice from the top of the wharf. "Hey you kids, want to earn a quarter?" They yelled "Yes." Putting on their shirts and pants (leaving their underwear for Rog's pillow) they climbed the ladder. The voice belonged to a fisherman they knew. He had delivery to make up in 'Gander Bay.' He did not have time to make it there. Would they be able to do it? Mike gave them the quarter and the fish and off they went. They ran all the way and delivered the fish. Now, here they were with a quarter to spend and the delight of deciding how to spend it. They had a wonderful time making the choice between ice cream or candy. The boys found out that they had enough money for both.

Another hour or so passed, Charlie and Harry's homing instinct kicked in. They leaped over hedges, played hide and seek and threw dirt clods at everything that looked like a target including neighborhood cats. They ran up the stairs to the house. Kelly was serving the boarders and they sat down quickly without even washing their hands. The boys were late and they did not want to call any special notice to them. That is until Kelly came in from the kitchen and eyed them. Where is little Rog? All the boarders stared at the kids. Harry and Charlie looked as if they did not know what she was talking about. Their blank looks attested to the fact that they had lost their minds or that they had eaten so much candy and ice cream that they were in a state of food shock. Perhaps it was momentary amnesia. The silence was deadly. Kelly had this strange look on her face. Again she spoke as if she could hardly believe she was saying it, "Harry and Charlie, where is your brother?" Poor Harry, stuttered, "I do not remember." Charlie, who had finally got his wits together, said softly as if he couldn't believe it himself, "Harry was just upset, he knows where Rog is. We left him down at the wharf," he added trying to be casual. "I'll go down and get him." Harry was crying now and the boarders all got up from the table and headed out the door with Kelly ahead of them. One of the O'Conner boys was walking his beat and joined them.

They could hear Rog's crying a street away and Kelly finally found him where the boys left him. He was sitting in the middle of the raft with his bottle in hand. His little face was bright pink from the sun and his bawling. The wharf was usually very busy; however, today was quiet and empty, except for the crowd now excitedly trying to get Rog up off the raft. Officer O'Connor went down the ladder, picked up the screaming boy, and was handed up from the people on each rung until he reached mom. Lots of shouts and hurrahs as they trooped home victorious from saving little Roger. Kelly sent for a couple of growlers of beer and boarders drank toasts to the sunburned babe.

I never did know what Kelly said to the two boys. I was not told. Harry and Charlie cried buckets mostly out of pure fright of what might have happened. I think any punishment or scolding they received was nothing in comparison to the absolute terror and fright they experienced. One thing they did have to go back to the wharf and pick up their underclothes and Roger's bottle.

Chapter 10—Kelly's Kosmetics

Kelly's hair and face care were strange as far as I was concerned. I went to a private Catholic school, wearing any embellishing formulas on my face or hair was not allowed. My Mother had her beauty treatment at a beauty salon and the only thing I remember her doing was her toenails. She always brushed her hair with care and great many strokes. I never paid much attention to any of it until I was introduced to Kelly's ways.

She had red hair and a good hearty shade of red. The color from her pictures looked to me like a cross from rust to a brighter shade but not carrot hued. It changed as she grew older and so with each henna treatment she varied the color as she pleased. Well, I had never seen anybody color their hair. She was like a sorceress mixing up a magic potion. She had a small saucer full of henna that she mixed with some liquid. The result was a muddy dark red. Out came the toothbrush and with a towel over her shoulder and a rubberized cap she would apply the mess to her hair inch by inch. It was fascinating to watch.

Sometimes, she diverted my attention from the work of her hands, by telling me that her hair had faded with the years. Not that it was getting gray or white, just that it was fading and she had to restore it to its former brilliance. The henna got over everything and the sink and the bathroom was a mess by the time she finished. When it was all done and she had washed her hair, it looked good. In fact, it looked as if that was her regular color. I could not remember what the color was before.

The finishing touches were her eyebrows. I never noticed them before. The fact was she did not have any. Kelly had plucked them all out at once and they never grew out. I half believed her story but I watched intently as she penciled them in. They were so even.

My father was dropping me off at her apartment one time and she answered the door looking like a ghost.

Dad said "Oh for Gods sakes you have gotten your mud pack on. You scared the hell out of me Ma"

"Oh Yocky," retorted Kell, "just got to look my best."

When it was time to wash it off, and the strange apparition that greeted us was Kelly once more. Later, after Dad left, I asked her what the stuff was on her face and she told me it was Fuller's earth and witch hazel. It was years later I tried it myself and surprised my girls. She was right it was refreshing and removed the wrinkles for a time. I learned so much about women from her, especially the beauty secrets.

She had a body like "Winnie-the Pooh," round and not unpleasant. Her little round belly and fanny reminded me always of a Walt Disney character, the cute little round animals he drew. When the work day was over, she always came home and immediately changed her clothes. What she got into was comical to me even as a youngster. She had a foam green night gown that reached a little below her knees and accentuated every roundness she had. With the creamy freckle skin, the red hair, plus the light green dumpling look, she was just cute. My father used to ask her why she wore the gown and she always answered that it was so comfortable. I can still see her sitting at the table, legs crossed at the ankles, in all her color with a beer in her hand.

Kelly was always barefooted when she came home and always complained of her feet hurting. In fact, she had two tremendous bunions that gave her problems. I remember her going to the hospital to have them treated for. She walked with her toes and her feet pointing outward with a sailor's swagger.

I always compared her to my mother's attire and style. There was no comparison to be made. Each one was so different. Both dressed very well and looked fantastic. The only secret was that Kelly did her own fashioning and beautifying, while Mom had the advantage of professional direction and help.

Chapter 11—Grammy's Florsheims

Grammy, as long as I could remember, wore rather strange shoes. I say strange because they did not fit the rest of her. She always wore a long flowered dress with a light soft colored pattern. There was usually lace at her neckline. A white apron girdled her middle and she looked very much like what she was, a granny. That is until you got to her feet. Then what she wore for shoes was completely incongruous. They were dark shiny large shoes that looked like men to me. Reminded me of a ballet dancer wearing army boots. It was very strange, and stranger still when on some days, she had white bucks or brown oxfords. I accepted these as time went by until one day she had on a pair of shiny patent leathers. I asked my mother about it and said they looked like Dad's dancing shoes. She laughed and said they were and looked good on her. I was puzzled and asked her why she was wearing Dad's shoes. What a story I got. Grammy was out on the porch saying her prayers and Mom began with a long introduction that was another story upon a story.

"Your grandmother was in her thirties, I guess and had three children. There was Stephan, the oldest, just starting his teens. Then there was Tomas, five years old, and the littlest was baby Elizabeth. There was an outbreak of Cholera in her village and it was taking a heavy death toll. The doctor died and then the priest did too. Grammy lost Stephan, then Tomas and the little one died in her arms as she waited for the new doctor to treat her. She was completely devastated and in a state of shock as she carried little Elizabeth back home and buried her. Her husband was home with a high fever and his future looked grim. It was the worst time in her life. She bathed his hot body and gave him some liquid. He was resting a bit more comfortably and so she went to the kitchen to see about a meal. The wood box was completely empty. Since Tomas was sick he hadn't been able to keep the box filled and she had been too busy with her dying children. It was the last straw. Her mind and body ached with the day and night care of them and all the tiredness and sorrow that attended. It was just about all she could handle. She went out to the wood pile and got the ax and began to chop. Grammy told Mom that she chopped five pieces and had split them. She took heart and began to split one more piece. Then she brought the ax down neatly between the big toe and the first little one on her right foot. She was horrified watching the blood spew forth. Grammy told mom that she didn't remember much pain at first and just wrapped her foot tightly with a clean cloth. She said she got the fire built, the soup ready and fed her husband. Tomas was a little better and did take some soup. The following days were miserable for her as the foot throbbed and ached. She dressed it and kept it clean. Hobbling around caring for Tomas who now was getting better. The deep wound healed miraculously. The foot was never the same of course. It healed, but was turned and twisted a bit as she had bound it. Shoes were a problem. But at least she and her husband were alive and well again.

I don't know what she used for shoes before my Dad married her daughter. I know that Dad's feet were not too big and somehow, someway it came to be that she would wear his cast-offs. It was a very good arrangement. He wore a size six or seven that gave her plenty of room for her damaged foot. She loved his shoes. He always bought the best quality and never really wore them out. He was rather vain about his appearance. So Grammy had quality men's footwear for all the years. My mother had a pair made especially for her and she used them for Sunday best. The rest of the time she wore her dashing Florsheims.

Chapter 12—The Gypsies

Roving Gypsy bands moved constantly over the Russian countryside. They obeyed no laws except the demands of their King. They were not welcomed with open arms. For survival they mended pans, and sold small articles. Horse trading and stealing was their major occupation when the opportunity presented itself. Grammy's husband Tomas had a lesson in the latter when he was offered a milk white horse, it was a magnificent animal. The price was reasonable. In fact it was so good, Tomas was a little suspicious but he was told by the owner that anyone who could keep up with his daughters' dancing deserved a fine horse. The night before at the gypsies' camp, there was much dancing and a prize was offered to the one who could out last his daughter. Tomas was spectacular and did succeed in wearing out the gypsy girl. The father said he would give him a prize the following day. This was his reward, this beautiful horse, and the money the man wanted was so little. The sale was finalized. Before the money left his hand, Tomas was told that the horse was only good for riding and would not pull the lightest carriage or shay. Tomas took the horse home with joy in his heart. Now he could take the family to church on Sunday and what a sight they would be. What a bargain he made. Grammy thought the beast was beautiful but she had reservations about breaking the horse to a carriage. She was still mad that he had been over to the gypsy's camp for half the night before.

The "wanderers" left as quick as they came and Tomas concentrated on training his beautiful horse. He was good with it and very patient. However anytime he hitched it to carriage, the horse would not move. Once he unhitched him and put a saddle on, his steed would wait until he mounted.

Then the two had a grand ride and "Beauty" pranced and galloped at his command. Again however when she was hitched up she would not move. At one point he whipped her to no avail and he was sorry, he had resorted to this manner of punishment. He was at his wits end. Grammy said she was at the point she did not care. The horse had taken just about all of Tomas' time and he was cranky. He finally decided to sell her. The next morning he was getting ready to go and he looked outside and saw his hired man sitting in the carriage. "Beauty" was hitched up and motionless.

There was a small fire under the belly of the horse. Old Jacob had set it hoping to make "Beauty" move. Grammy and Tomas watched in pure horror. There was nothing to do now but wait. The fire was already licking at her white belly. Then with lightning reaction she charged away from the flames and ran at a high gallop between two aspens. Unfortunately there was room for her but none for the carriage. She was hurt quite badly and so was Old Jacob. The carriage was completely destroyed. The next few months were spent nursing both hired man and "Beauty." Both recovered and the horse was sold. Grammy twitted him about his dancing with the gypsies and said the next time he would not be so lucky.

Chapter 13—The Baptism

Now Kelly was extremely religious. Her rosary beads hung on the bed post for her nightly recitation and on special days she started out with devotion. Her little apartment bedroom had a very nice picture of the "Savior" on the wall opposite the bed. It was a well-known painting of Christ with his hand pointing to his heart. I remember it well because when I stayed there, she would let me put the little light on that was attached to the frame. It was sort of a night light and kept me from bad dreams.

Sundays were burdensome. Kelly had to be on time for the nine o'clock Mass no matter what. Nothing but death would have kept her from St. Vincent's church. In that case she would have been there anyway albeit a little late. Breakfast was always gluey oatmeal which I loaded up with sugar when she wasn't looking. Watching her get ready for church was a fascinating experience. Her sea green nightdress over the Winnie the Pooh figure disappeared into the bedroom. I was not allowed to be present for the unmentionables, yet they consisted of a heavy corset that that fitted like a glove. While I waited for her to emerge, I plinked on the piano until she told me that was enough. Then she sort of drifted in to the living room looking like one of those dancer pictures of the 1890 girls putting on the rest while she asked me questions about our family. Kelly's bunions challenged her stockings. Her feet were like two misshapen potatoes, and the stockings had to be carefully pulled over the bumps and corns. After the shoes, I always helped with the dress closures just because I was there and it was during one of these sessions that a story popped out about her religious "shenanigans."

Her youngest son, my uncle Rog had a little boy and the family rejoiced. The mother Dorothy was Scotch Presbyterian and had remained so, even though Kelly had exhorted her to join the "true faith." She tried to persuade Dorothy to baptize the child Catholic. Well, her daughter-in law said she would be in charge of her child's religion and would tolerate no interference. In explaining herself, she said,

"Well Jeannie, Dorothy had no right to keep the 'true faith' from my grandchild. I told her so. Your uncle has been very, very mad at me for saying anything. It's a shame he didn't marry a good Catholic girl. There would be no trouble like this."

I said, "What trouble——Kell? I haven't heard of any." She smiled at me and gave a laugh.

"Oh, there's no trouble now at all. Roger is in the church and it's over with. Did you brush your teeth?"

I knew she wanted to stop the conversation so I went in and put some toothpaste on my finger and rubbed it fast over my teeth. Then I made some gargling noises so she'd think I was really working hard. The phone rang and I came out to hear her saying;

"Now Yockie (her nickname for my father)...don't say that to your mother!"

"Of course I had a party..."

"....Yes when you and Jeanne had gone away with Roger and Dot."

"Uh-huh. St. Vincent's. I gave him the baptismal name of Patrick."

"....That's not nice to say. I just did it for the child's sake. My cousin, Delia was the Godmother and John O'Connell was Godfather."

"....They never asked. Guess they figured you knew all about it."

"....Don't get so upset. Father Lynch did it. I didn't tell him anything. Just a little soul waiting to come into the Church."

"....Stop yelling at me or I'm going to hang up. This is no way to treat your mother!"

Kelly slammed down the phone. I stood there open mouthed, my grandmother was fighting with my Dad. I never saw this before. Kell was pink...I suppose her blood pressure was in full bloom. She stayed near the phone and told me to get her pocketbook. a monstrous black satchel, and to make the bed. While I was in the bedroom, the phone rang again. I stopped everything. I didn't want to miss a thing.

"Yes," (in a quiet even voice that I rarely heard Kelly use)

"I'll accept your apology."

"Yockie don't take it so hard."

"She'll get over it. I mean her no harm."

Then in a more conciliatory voice; "How did you hear about it?"

"...The Mckennas..."

"....Yes, I knew they had a good time."

"After the priest left, things really got going."

"The police came over to tell us to tone it down."

"Molly Wansboro's boy.nice fellow."

"Oh Harry, no I don't want to cause a rift in the family."

"Let's wait awhile."

"Maybe by the time the holidays are here she'll calm down."

"Hey, little Rog sure got a lot of presents."

"Delia's going to bring them down to the office."

"Don't dare to bring them up to Rog's house."

"There's $150.00 and a lot of special gifts."

"Maybe that'll make them feel better."

"Oh, I had at least a hundred people. It was a great party."

"Didn't even break anything and had a couple of the gals clean up for us."

"You know the Maguire sisters."

"They clean offices in New York, and came up for the celebration."

"Oh, they're fine…"

"Haven't seen you since little Harry's Baptism."

"….Are you coming over this afternoon?"

"….Ok, I won't speak of it. Are we going out for Sunday dinner?"

"…Good, see you then."

Kelly and I went to eleven o'clock mass and Dad picked us up for dinner. It was like nothing had happened to ruffle anybody's feelings. I enjoyed myself.

Chapter 14—Another Wolf Story

Grammy had another wolf story that was a hair raiser. My mother told me this one first and Grammy verified it. I think she told me beforehand because it was rather indelicate. I must say the way Grammy told the story made chuckle.

It had to do with her village in the old country, a neighbor of hers and a wolf pack. She was very vain and proud, lording over her friends and acquaintances. Her husband was a hunter and a trapper. The fortunes of the family had become sizable because of his abilities. Her pride was a long fur coat with a great hood made from the many different kinds of animals he had shot or trapped. The tailor of the village had carefully pieced them all together in a pleasing pattern and style. It truly was a beautiful coat and kept her warm in the desperate cold of the long winter. It was the talk of the village.

One day she went visiting at the estate showing off her magnificent coat and found herself starting home later than she should. The dusk was upon her as she hurried through the woods and snow. As I said in the other story, nighttime in the forest is dangerous because of wild animals. But in winter, when the game is scarce, it is fool hardy to venture past the security of the village because of roving wolf packs.

As she rushed along the sleigh ruts, she thought she saw gray shapes among the bare thickets. "Perhaps it is my imagination" she said. "I'm scared and I think I see things." She pulled the coat around her tightly and its warmth settled her rampant fears. The dusk turned to a gray gloom with only the brightness of the white snow relieving the onrush of night. If there was any doubt as to the nature of those gray forms, it was removed because eyes were part of each shape, bright and flashing, she counted at least eight wolves. She continued hurrying and staring with fascinating horror at her would be the executioners. Her life would be forfeit to their hungry jaws. They kept abreast of her always at a distance using the thickets as a cover. Her mind became very clear as she estimated her chances of survival. Perhaps she could keep walking and gain the village before they pounced on her. Moving even faster and out of the fold of her hood she saw they were keeping up.

"Closing in for the kill," she thought. Her feet were moving automatically, but with greater effort now. Her mind was concentrating on one thing, her survival. She shuddered as she struggled on. It was dark, and she realized that perhaps there was a mile left to go toward the open land to the village. Maybe she could make it. She was exhausted. Then her foot slipped and she sank into the snow. With terror, she saw the pack leader running towards her. She threw the hood over her head and curled up tightly under the great coat. It was all over for her now and she didn't want to see the end. There she lay huddled into a soft fur ball. The silence was almost complete. The heavy coat kept out sound and the dark was merciful.

Time seemed endless…and it was quiet….so quiet. Her breathe was in little short gasps and the only comfort was that she still was breathing. Nothing was happening…no vicious tearing or growling. The snow was an absorbing cushion for sound and her coat was too. She thought she heard a sniffing sound. Then there was nothing except the sound of her own pulsating body and breathing. She waited tensely and horror struck for the most certain end. Then there was a sound she couldn't identify…a soft tattoo of sound…a silence again. Sniffing and another soft tattoo repeated itself. The wolves were marking the coat. With relief her mind pieced together the answer for this strange behavior. The coat was made of many animal skins that probably confused the leader. Also, the human odor was securely encased within the great coat. There was no other smell to the "creature" lying in the snow except the subtle smells of many animals long since dead. The leader decided it wasn't anything worthwhile to eat. He cocked his leg against it and trotted off. In turn, each of the wolves did the same. The soft tattoo stopped and she waited a long time, mentally saying prayers of thanksgiving for the deliverance from a terrible end. She peeked out from the furs. The stars were out and the pack had gone. She took off the coat and shook as much of the urine off, wiped it in the snow and put it back on. She hurried with renewed strength towards the village for safety.

The anticlimax to the story was startling and almost fatal. As the woman approached the village, the dogs set up a frenzy of barking and rushed out to meet her. They caught the odors from her coat. Galvanized into action by the smell of wolves and danger, they tore into her. Her cries and shrieks brought the men who beat off the dogs and brought her to safety. Her coat was in shreds but she escaped serious injury and certain death again because the coat had protected her from the slashing fangs of the dogs.

Chapter 15—Kelly's Companions

Kelly always had a friend with her. It was probably due to growing up with her sister Josephine in a close sister relationship. Jo didn't look too much like Kelly and had dark hair and didn't share the laughter of life but she was a wonderful buddy for Kelly. When it came to arguing either with each other or Pete, (Jo's husband,) it was a battle of semantic skills or the winner was usually Kelly. The girls truly enjoyed each others company. I think Peter put it crudely when one day he remarked to Dad. "Those two are closer than the cheeks of my ____. I love my wife and Kelly, but those two together is more than anyone could handle." When they went down to the bar, both of them would sing and play the piano. This was their world, and their husbands were not part of it. Pete had a weight problem and didn't leave the house much after his retirement while "Shorty "was ailing and in a sanitarium, So the two made their own amusement and enjoyment. It was tragic went Josephine died suddenly. I think it was a heart attack. Kelly was so alone.

Her sister-in law visited from Long Island and relieved some of the lonesomeness. She had a gold topped cane and limped because of a hip problem. Mae was a picture of a dowager queen. She usually wore a black bombazine dress that reached to the floor. It was high necked with a little relief of lace at the top, and directly in the middle was a beautiful oval cameo. Mae had the voice of a crow, not to be disrespectful but her voice was shrill and crackling. Her hair piled high on her head completed the appearance of a grand lady. I'd visit and was in complete awe of her. I never knew who she was talking about. It was my Dad's side of the family and Kelly's in laws.

Mae tossed down the brandy as Kelly drank her beer and listened. They'd get to laughing so hard "You are so funny Mae, tell me some more about......." and they'd both laugh again. Mae loved Kelly very very much and when she died, she left Kelly a small chamois bag of yellow canary diamonds which Kelly treasured for the rest of her life. She showed them to me and I was impressed.

A few years later my father rented a small apartment above his offices to a refined seamstress named Melanie. It wasn't any time at all before she and Kelly were close friends, and we somehow were Melanie's family. She was a shy reserved little lady and Kelly took it upon herself to show her what her routine was. Melanie loved it. She made wonderful hats for Kelly and dresses to match. Kelly became a fashion plate and Melanie her devoted seamstress and mentor. The days were very happy for both. Dabbling in real estate now she was earning some money and was able to indulge herself. Melanie guided her through some of the formalities of business. Unfortunately for all the war broke out. My father left never to return as he died in Walter Reed hospital from a heart attack, I had gone into the military service and so had my brother. Kelly was with her youngest son Rog. Melanie, I think, left Albany to be with relatives, Kelly again was without a companion for a time.

Her last drinking buddy and conversationalist was my stepmother's father. My father after his divorce remarried again. The marriage lasted but five months before he died. I came back after eighteen months in the WACs and lived with my stepmother. Her father came to live with us. It didn't take long before "Kelly and Pop," were enjoying the pub up the street together. Kelly lived just a few blocks from us and as she said the walk did her good. I can still see them strolling along. Kelly in an animated conversation and Pop nodding in agreement. This was her last alliance. I think both of them went within a few years of each other.

Chapter 16—Kelly's Babysitting

There's nothing like spending a month or so with some body to realize how much you like that person, especially if you're a child and the person is your grandmother. I learned much about Kelly when she took care of us. Our parents went to California and Kelly took care of us for a month. What a wonderful time my brother and I had. It was like joining a circus. There was no rigid hard fast rules, except for coming home right after school, and going to nine o'clock Mass on Sundays. Everything else fell in line behind those two dicta. Delightfully our menu changed from, soups, stews and roasts to simpler fare. We had custard, baked beans, rice pudding chicken on Sunday, baked potatoes, and fish in between She served lettuce and tomatoes as a salad with our supper (always with vinegar and oil dressing.) She was always heavy on the vinegar. Breakfast was always oatmeal milk and toast. Lunch was always a sandwich. Supper was served at five instead of seven or eight, so we had time to play outside. This was so different for us. It was so much fun to play hide and seek with the neighborhood gang. Kelly would drink her beer and watch us from the sun room.

Some nights when there was nobody out, we'd sing to Kelly's piano playing. I learned all the "Gay-Nineties" songs and Broadway tunes. After that she would tell a story or two. These I didn't like because they were babyish. The "Woofy Dog" and the "Furry Cat" did keep Harry's interest until he fell asleep on the couch. We were never allowed to lie down on the couch, and I had a smidgen of guilt when he did it, but it didn't last long. What freedom we had, Kelly listened to my prayers every night and taught me few more too.

Wine was not a part of our life but one summer when Kelly was caring for us, we were introduced to the wine making industry. It seemed she had a recipe that was flawless and fantastic. Harry and I were enlisted to harvest the dandelions. We both thought it was great fun especially since quite a few adults were doing it too, I don't even recall all the details except that there was so much excitement and laughter to it. Eventually the wine was made and we had company all the time. I didn't know the people. They were all Kelly's friends and they were a merry lot. Harry and I had an ample chance to taste the product as well. It was different than what we were used too and we didn't much care for it. But Harry and I had our own party so to speak. With the winery going full blast and all the people saying how well behaved we were, nickels and dimes were pressed in our hands. They always told us to put it in our bank. The school banking program never saw a penny of it. We bought more candy from "Bachelors" (candy/grocery store) during that time than we had in months.

Aside from the wine making business we just had fun with her. The weekends were filled with trips to the fields or the park. One time she helped us build a tree house. It wasn't very good, but we were happy with the efforts. She picked wild flowers with us and went to the swamp to inspect its inhabitants. She never minded wet feet or muddy clothes. That wasn't like the adults we knew. The place was hopping on the weekends. Cousins we didn't know came, and we played and played until we and our playmates finally fell asleep on somebody caring laps. The days sped by and the wonder and magic of it all came to an abrupt end, Dad and Mom came home. Time for children can be an eternity or far too short. It was far too short, and our holiday ended suddenly.

Here was Dad and Mom and indeed we did miss them. There were lonesome times that crept in at night——-and there were those loving arms we missed Hugs and kisses and tears were genuine, and mixed feeling were added when we hugged Kelly good-bye. It was a delicate balance.

The story about the dandelion wine slipped out and Mom was in full battle dress ready to take on Kelly. I think Harry told her what fun it was in his childish way. Dad was the interrogator and the tales of our adventure came forth. Kelly acquitted herself well and brought the event into some perspective that was acceptable. The other times she took care of us were under scrutiny as well. Questions on our schedule and how we were cared for were subjects were up for discussion. Both Harry and I said things were just fine. Eventually Mom extracted some detail that put Kelly on the"bad" list. Time and reason cures all things. Kelly did mind us again much to our delight.

Chapter 17—The Charmer

Grammy had a way with her that was delightful. I wasn't too sure what it was except perhaps it was the wonderful feeling I when I had when I was with her. There was a magical warmth and fondness that seemed to radiate from her. When I came home from school and she was visiting for the winter I could hardly wait to see her. I'd kiss her and touch the rosary, she held in her hands. I was her Janina (little Jeanne). She always fed me well and took care of me. She would clean up my room, sew on buttons and take care of my laundry.

Later after I told her what I did in school, she would tell me little stories as I sat on the floor with my head in her lap. They were very special times. Looking back I can remember she was the one who taught me how to tie my shoes long time ago. Sitting on the old cedar chest with me, she patiently instructed me in the art of the loop. My mother had a bad time with me and Grammy took over with her infinite patience. I think the caring she had, was the key.

Grammy was not just a patient old lady, weighed down by all the years and caring, she was funny. We'd get laughing over some little thing and have a merry time. It could be anything from a silly movie she saw with my father or something that happened. Anyway she was a friend to laughter and we enjoyed each other. I wasn't the only one who enjoyed her. My father was enchanted with her. I was more than a little bit puzzled here was a lady in her eighties and my father in his late thirties. He wanted to be with her, and take her out. When she came to town and he would call my mother up and arrange a date with Grammy. Mom and Dad were separated at the time and family tensions ran high. Didn't seem to matter at all. She would be all dressed up in one of her flowered dresses, and good shoes. He'd drive up in his convertible and away they'd go. Dinner would be over and the dusk coming on when the two showed up again. She had a big bouquet of flowers, usually gladiolas if they were in season. She had supper and he bought her a big ice-cream cone which she was finishing. Dad would take her to the door, ring it, and wait for mom to answer. After telling Mom what they did and where they went, he'd give Grammy a little peck on the cheek and leave. While she was visiting, the two of them took in movies at least once a week. He would come up in the afternoon, leaving his law practice, and the two of them would sneak down to the old Leland Theatre and watch cowboy movies or comedies. She'd come home full of candy ice-cream, and popcorn. This continued until Dad went into the military service right after Pearl Harbor.

Dad died in service and I went down to the farm to see her, after I had joined the Woman's Army Corps. She showed me the little altar she had made for Dad in her bedroom. His military picture was flanked with votive candles and there were fresh flowers in a little vase. A rosary draped over the frame and an American flag to the side completed the scene. I hugged her and the tears filled both our eyes. I gave her a picture of me in uniform and it joined the tableau.

I married Bill after the war and as a young couple we shared our lives and history. I spoke of both grandmothers with an intensity that brought them into a clear focus. All the good times and all the help they'd been. Different for each, but with reverence and thankfulness for the parts they had played in my life. Grammy was now in her nineties. I just had my first baby and she came to visit and to stay. Well she stayed about a month. Bill was just as enchanted with her as Dad was before. Again there was that language barrier but it didn't matter a whit. He asked me if I thought it would be alright to take her for a ride in the afternoon. My heart and mind did a flip backwards and I remembered Dad and her years before. Well everyday she was here, he took her out. Yes, she came home eating an ice-cream cone too. Grammy was a little feeble and unable to read the Polish newspaper he bought her everyday. But she never let him know it. When she left, Bill hugged and kissed her with much feeling. He never did see her alive after that and he cried quietly at her wake.

I learned what her charm was. She had those attractive traits in a person that can calm, and soothe you, and still be spirited and lively. Having nothing to do with her age, her delightful ways were pleasing and infused me with loving care.

Chapter 18—Pizza Patient

I was in the hospital for a gastric upset and they were running a series of tests on me. I was at the stage were the hospital life was quite comfortable. I had no more upset and was hoping I could go home. I don't recall any hordes of visitors so I just sat propped up in my bed, waiting for something to happen. It did and Kelly was the messenger of all the goods things. In she bounced with her friend Melanie. Both were dressed up stylishly with very fashionable dresses and Tuscany straw hats and all the accessories. They were walking advertisements to Melanie's skill as a seamstress; Kelly had a black suitcase that she carried with difficulty.

At the same time, a nurse came in to check my temp and take my blood pressure. "The girls" looked on with interest and Melanie said "How is she?' The nurse smiled, "Oh, she fine now. She'll probably go home as soon as the doctor sees her." Kelly watched her retreat from the room and she went to the door and closed it. But before she shut it she called softly to the nurse,"Is it all right to keep the door closed, we just want to visit a bit without interruption. I'm her grandmother and the other lady is her grand aunt. We're visiting from out of town." This was a first for me, her saying she was a grandmother to me and as for Melanie being my grandaunt that was a delightful thought.

Here we were the three of us I jumped out of bed and hugged them both. Then Kelly and Melanie lifted the suitcase onto the bed and opened it. The rich aroma of pizza filled all the corners of the sterile smelling room. Watching them unwrap the items of this treasure chest was evident that a large pizza was lying in the bottom. Comforted and held in place by a box with layers of wax paper and a tablecloth. On the other side lay three goblets each enveloped by a large linen napkin. All of the contents were arranged on the tray table on my bed. Then the surprise came. From Kelly's enormous pocket book appeared a quart of beer. I laughed till the tears ran down my face.

"Kelly, how did you ever manage that beer?"

"It wasn't easy. I had to take out all my personal papers, and just about all my cosmetics except for lipstick and my wallet. Nice fit don't you think?"

About an hour later, there was just an empty pizza box and an empty beer bottle that was returned to the pocketbook. The goblets were rinsed and dried with the napkins and the tablecloth was company for the rest of the wrappings. The room was immaculate as it was before except for an occasional breathe of pizza that was floating along with the smell of the malt.

What a grand time we had. Kelly regaled me with stories of the McGuiness sisters, friends of hers from New York and the antics they indulged in when cleaning the suites in the sky-scrapers at night. Melanie added stories of her youth when her family were very wealthy and the had a magnificent villa they had in Italy. The afternoon wore on and finally as the shadows lengthened, I became sleepy with all the pizza and beer visiting my empty stomach, there was a knock on the door and the nurse came in.

"You must have had a great time judging from all the laughter coming from this room. I didn't have the heart to interrupt. I'm going off duty now and I think its time for you "Miss" to rest awhile before dinner."

"The Girls" left quickly but not before giving me some hugs and kisses. And it reminded me not to talk when the nurse came close to take my temp, pulse, or blood pressure. My stomach felt wonderful, and the doctor was pleased. I don't remember whether I ever told him of the beer and pizza. I just felt that was what I needed, with some laughter and caring.

Chapter 19—The Raggedy A—Cadets

Kelly's husband was a platinum hairdo chap about 5"6', appropriately named "Shorty." An amiable man, with a wealth of humor and knowledge, he was a good sparring partner for his wife. They fought their battles of words with tenacity and skill. There was one item they waged war over and over and over. It was religion. She of course was a devout Catholic and he was Baptist. They were married in the Catholic Church however and when the children came along, she raised them Catholic. All this happened after monumental battles, and Kelly had emerged as victor. However, the skirmishes weren't over. When Kelly wanted to enroll them all in parochial schools, new battles erupted. This time Shorty was the winner. The boys went to public school. This did not preclude them from serving on the altar on Sundays. She won that concession.

The oldest one Charlie graduated and left home, and Harry, my dad, was floundering through his Junior year. The letters from the Principal were red flags that Harry wouldn't be graduating with his class the following year. Shorty wasn't over concerned with this state of affairs. After all he had been educated at home by his mother. She was a school teacher before she married, and gave him the benefit of her learning. He had a broad education in the classics, Latin Greek and French literature, and Philosophy plus the regular courses. He saw no reason why he couldn't teach his son. Well, Kelly wasn't so sure. Her third grade education was no match for his. But she had the benefit of a lively intellect polished by her life in Gander Bay and she was intuitive where it came to her sons.

She had a mother-son talk with Harry about his grades, and then went over to Christian Brothers Academy. It was a Catholic semi-military school. Bright uniforms and Academic excellence, the Brother took great care in turning out students who were ready for college. Kelly with the gift of expression and earnestness prevailed on the Brothers. Whatever she said is lost to memory, but that coming fall, Harry was enrolled as a cadet. His father had not made any move towards teaching Harry at home. He was inclined to let things pass.

From what both my Dad and Kelly told me, he had a very difficult time those first three months. One brother, Father Parelin took special care with him and threw Harry into a hard line study and tutoring program. He monitored him in every facet of his school life. It paid off and he was becoming an excellent student. Kelly was ecstatic.

Christian Brothers Academy or C.B.A. as it was called marched in all the city parades. They were a very impressive sight coming up State Street with their band ahead and robed "brothers" marching along side. The crowds always cheered. At the end of their band lines they were a small group of youngsters who had no uniforms, but nonetheless were marching along. They were enrolled at the academy but did not have money enough to buy their uniforms.

Shorty was walking up the street when the Armistice Day parade was in full swing. He had a bunch of his cronies with him and they were chitchatting. He saw the last group of boys from the Academy and shouted. "There go the raggedy ass cadets." After his outburst, one of his buddies yelled

"Hey Shorty, there's Harry, third one in the first column." Sure enough there was his son, eyes-straight ahead, marching along with a stern and defiant look on his face. The sneer on Shorty's face had changed to complete surprise and bewilderment. Another of his friends said.

"I didn't know you sent your boy to the academy. How come he doesn't have his uniform? Did you just order it?"

Shorty managed to get his sneers, surprise, and embarrassment and now pride all together, and under control. He answered.

"His uniform is on order." The lie was soothing to his psyche.

It didn't take much time to get home. Even though he had to go to the seminary first to meet with his teachers for the first time. They were accommodating, considering it was a legal holiday. It didn't take much time to make arrangement for the uniform, and he paid for it on the spot. Despite his protest about the Papacy, and the religion he was favorably impressed. Kelly was waiting for him when he got home and was ready for a joust. She was furious about his comments. Mrs. Kennedy had been at the parade and told her what was said. He completely defused her rage after he told her he got Harry his uniform. But she was still fuming that he had called the boys "The raggedy ass cadets." The rest of Harry's Senior year was a tribute to the school's effort with him. He graduated with honors and marched in full dress uniform in every parade.

Kelly had her way, but she was still miffed about the whole incident. The two never solved their differences about religion, even after death. She wanted to be buried in consecrated ground and was buried in St. Agnes Cemetery. Shorty was buried in an adjoining cemetery with a fence separating them.

Chapter 20—Grammy's Uncles

In the back parlor of the old farmhouse was a faded picture that seemed to come out of a book of pirates or some wild novel. There were two men dressed in Cossack uniforms with huge sabers. They looked like scimitars to me. Huge mustaches covered their upper lips and draped down the serious faces. I was a little frightened by the picture, and asked my mother who they were. She told me they were Grammy's uncles and promised to tell me about them, on the way home from our visit.

Once in the car, I asked her again and she began the tales. First she told me they had joined the Cossack school at Petrograd when they were about fourteen and sixteen years of age. After two years of training, they were part of the regular Cossacks. They were sent to Vladivostok, the far southeastern end of the Russia, to spend some time there. When they were finally able to return, it took them two years to make the trek homeward. I shall call them Jon and Patrice, because their names are lost in my memory. The family was kept in much awe and wonderment of the many stories Jon would tell of the East. It was a little like Marco Polo coming back to Italy with tales. Mother said the whole village was buzzing with comments. Patrice was by nature a farmer, and in his travels he carefully saved seed of different plants and vegetables so they could be planted at home. Some of their braver villagers took the seeds and planted them in the spring. Most of vegetables grew and were tried and liked enough to save the seed for the following year. There was one exception. The first tomato that ever grew in that place in Poland scared the wits out of the peasants. It was red, bright red and had a fuzzy stem. It also had a different smell than the other plants. No one dared to eat it. Patrice showed them how to cook tomatoes and ate them raw for his suspicious neighbors. Nobody would try it because of its bright color. It was red; therefore a vegetable of the devil and it should not be eaten. The villagers decided that all the tomato plants should be burned immediately. It was done. Unfortunately Patrice's house caught on fire as well. There were many who thought that poor Patrice was doing the work of the devil and he was justly punished. My mother never told me if the two stayed in the village. I think not. They probably went back to Petrograd where the ignorance was at a lower level.

I did ask about those wicked swords and whether they were actually used. My mother affirmed that they had had much use and Jon and Patrice had very strong arms from doing so.

Chapter 21—Kelly's Electioneering

Kelly always generated her own excitement and had a lot of fun doing it. The local bars, where she had been known for years were her arenas of activity. Her father owned a bar and she had worked in her father's establishment before and after he died. Her gift of gab was superb, and her manner was friendly and easy. She enjoyed the company. Kelly played a terrific piano. Gay Nineties numbers, all the Irish ballads and a lusty Ragtime were her forte. After she sipped a drink or two she took over the piano and the place livened up considerably. Voices were raised in the spirit of companionship of song. She could play anything after hearing it sung the first time. Kelly would make her visits as the spirit moved her and she was always welcome.

During one period of time Dad had political ambitions and was running for public office, in fact for awhile it seemed he always was. He was a Republican in a Democratic stronghold. I remember him running for District Attorney and City Court Judge. The format and the results were always the same. He had a truck with a PA. System on the back. The strains of McNamara's Band coming down the street were interspersed with a Vote for Dad. It was such an exciting time for all of us. I was in school and heard the tune knowing the truck was passing by with all the red and white bunting waving off its sides. He always lost the nomination which was predictable, yet there always seemed to be that hope which energized us all.

Anyway, to get back to Kelly, she was having a ball. What excitement in her life. She was so proud of her son. She enjoyed much attention from all her friends, distant relatives and her friends at the taverns. Of course it follows that somebody would always call Dad and tells him that his mother was down at the Lark St. Tavern or some other hangout. This was not a good public image and it was imperative that he get her home, Pop would leave in a rush.

I heard about what happened from the tremendous arguments that followed.

The bar was hopping by the time Dad got there with music, beer and laughter. She was in her glory. Dad was patient and tried to explain his argument for her to come home with him. He told her to think of his campaign and what a poor image she was making for him. Here was a campaigner's mother playing in a bar and drinking beer. All hell would break loose. Kelly lived up to her red hair, her Irish wit and her defiance. After a joust of words, Dad suggested that she maybe should come home in an hour or so. Well Kelly treated that as a victory and suggested that he have a drink with her and a song or two. Then he could drive her home. Well he was a chip off the old block, and sang the songs they knew so well together. He knew all the words having learned them from Kelly as a child. The night was delightful Dad had sung many songs and did a little campaigning to boot. I often thought he got more votes from these gatherings than he did from other sections of the populace.

Chapter 22—Celebration of the Onion

Grammy was a fine cook, at least in my estimation. When she came up from the country to spend some of the harsh winter with us, she spoiled me with her home made bread. I remember coming home from school and could smell the baking a block away. Between the raisin bread and the prune bread, I gained weight. One of my other favorite meals was potato pancakes. I ate them until I could hardly move from the table. No matter what I wanted she would oblige. From stews to Polish sausage, pea soup, and little sweets, my days were series of delights in her cookery.

The winter days were short and snowy, and the warmth of the kitchen was a focal point. The Christmas holidays and New Years celebration were the highlights and then we all settled in for the long gray time. That is, everybody but Grammy. She would pick out a nice full onion, and place it carefully in a flower pot filled with dirt. I do not know where she got the dirt. Maybe Mom got it for her someplace. Anyway the onion and its pot had the place of honor above the kitchen sink. It did not take too long for a little green sprout to creep out of its confines. We, at least the women in the house, watched it grow and against the background of the white mounded landscape of the yard, it was a picture of defiance. I always asked mom what Grammy was saying as she watered the little sprout.

Mom laughed and said, "It's an old expression she has said from the time I was a little girl in Poland. I suppose it was a hope for the renewal of the earth. Translated, she says "After Christmas it's spring" I think it's a wonderful thought."

Through the years, it has popped into my head. The winters were fine for all the winter sports and I enjoyed them, but I got impatient for the spring and growing things. This quote gave me the hope and a little burst of joy that truly the onion was right in growing. Because after Christmas, there was the belief that spring was coming not far behind.

After Christmas, it's Spring

After Christmas, it's Spring
The short gray days of winter
stretch shadows o'er my mind,
And even though there's holidays
I'd leave it all behind.

For I hate the cold,
the sleet and snow
The grisly temp of 20 below.
I long for the warmth of May,
and then I remember,
that AFTER CHRISTMAS, IT'S SPRING.

Never mind the snow,
it will all go.
The flowers will bloom
in spite of the gloom.
The trees are bare,
but I don't care,
because
the joys of May and June
in my memory sing
so in my heart I know
AFTER CHRISTMAS, IT'S SPRING.

You mean all this will go,
After Auld Lang Syne?
And a bye to Santa's ring
Yes you have to forget the woe
of winter's bluster and blow
There's violets in the woods
beneath the blanket of snow
and the gardens hold a promise
of crocuses waiting below.

So forget the ache of the cold
the bite of winter's wing
and say farewell to all that
and sing
AFTER CHRISTMAS, IT'S SPRING.

Chapter 23—Epilogue

Both of my grandmothers died within two years of each other. Kelly went first and Grammy's passed on the following spring. Here is a short review of their passing. Some have asked me whether they ever met, if they did what was their reaction. Did they like each other? Did they ever go out together? Just what was their relationship?

I remember the first time they did met at a family gathering. I don't even recall the circumstances. Any way they were very polite to each other. Grammy didn't speak much English in her best days, so communication was hard. I know both greeted each other warmly and my mother did some interpretation. They sat together as I recall, with Mom doing the translating. Each was trying very hard. Later on, Grammy said to me" Was that Kelly's real hair?

I told her that Kelly touched it up and she smiled. She had many questions about her dress and make-up and age. Well I helped with everything but the age. From time to time she was very inquisitive about Kelly's life and her work and seemed quite awed by her. I think she saw Kelly as the modern woman and wanted to know what she did with her days. The idea of working in the outside world was foreign to her and her curiosity was thoroughly aroused. Kelly on the other hand was just as inquisitive about Grammy.

Why she didn't speak English? How old was she. And then she would say,"She must have had a hard life." I told her all knew about Grammy and she listened very carefully, asking questions in between my stories. I had the distinct feeling that Kelly had her mixed into some fairy tales of long ago, when the ladies all wore their hair up in a bun, a long dresses and an apron. They were always were baking cookies and treats for her children and lived next to a dark forest filled with wolves and magic.

It was sad that there was not enough conversation between them. I'm sure they would have enjoyed each other tremendously. Both were so different, yet the sameness of heart for their families and the efforts both made for their children gave them common ground. The language was the barrier. Each year, Grammy drifted into speaking Polish most of the time. She assumed now that I knew her tongue and in a way I did. By her gestures and tone I got the gist of what she said.

I do know this, the respect each had for the other was so evident, especially when leaving after a visit. They would hug each other. Grammy would say in English "Good bye," with her Polish accent and Kelly's smile would match hers.

Chapter 24—Kelly's Last Party

Kelly died as she lived, in a bit of a rush. She went into the hospital for a routine operation. A few more items unscheduled were excised, a blood clot formed in her lungs and she went very quickly.

Her wake was grand as these things go. She was "laid out" in the living room bay window, dressed in royal purple. The "old-timers—Irish All," remarked how well she looked and she did indeed. She had a look on her face that was rather regal. I had never seen this before. Moving and animated she now was solemn and still.

The McGinnis ladies, who cleaned offices at night in New York City, came all the way up to Albany to say "good-bye." They came in all snowy and cold and wanted to see "Kelly." Kneeling and praying over the coffin. Both hurried to the kitchen for a few belts to ward off the chill and the evil spirits. They were funny at the table telling all, with a light brogue, how the two grew up together and the good times they had. They told a host of tales of their hi-Jinx before they were married. They had all of us laughing so hard that the other relatives came in from the dining room to relieve their solemnity. It turned out to be quite a party, spreading its warmth and laughter. I felt Kelly was joining us, especially when they began the monologues and toasts to her and putting their glasses on the bier.

Anecdotes and charming stories of her escapades lightened the loss. Each, in turn, had something to say for the deceased and it all added a new perspective to her life. Her church appearance and graveside obsequies were solemn and quiet. It occurs to me now that perhaps they all had terrific headaches and hangovers from the celebration the night before. It had temporarily stilled their spirits.

Chapter 25—Grammy's Last Good-Bye

Grammy just faded away. I went down to the Catskill after she had a stroke. Her daughter-in-law Nora was taking wonderful care of her. Grammy was comatose. A short time later, she died without waking up. She just drifted off. Until the stroke she was able to be up and about although she had some problems. The family believed that if you could get Grammy back in her garden, after the long hard Catskill winter she would be fine. At ninety-six, she was busy digging and planting. In June, she died and her garden was in bloom.

Her funeral was a country affair. The old farmhouse was filled with her two children, grandchildren and her great grandchildren. The back parlor, all stiff and formal and used only for important occasions was now opened. The horse hair seats and the piano in the far corner looked so prim and proper. Grammy was in her coffin, in the middle of the room, on two wooden horses.

The children were playing tag and running around. At one point, a little boy put his hand up and patted his Grandma saying "Bye Grammy, and off he ran, being chased by his cousins. The last time Grandma was up and around when I visited, I recall all the little ones clustered near her as she sat at the table. One was repeating my actions from long ago. He had his head on her lap and she was stroking him. I think it was the same little fellow saying "good-bye" at her wake.

Her cortege was started by her grandson-in-laws, grandsons and her son taking her coffin down the steep hill to the waiting hearse. The day was warm with the whisper of growing things. As we trudged down the hill, there was no sadness, no sorrow, just the recognition of her life coming to a close. At the graveside, our committing her to the ground was an offering to God, of a soul that had lived long and well.

Printed in the United States
99189LV00003B/261/A

9 781424 197545